characterfirst.
education

elementary
curriculum

Self-Control

This curriculum offers approximately 3 hours of instruction, divided into 3 sections. Each section can be broken into smaller pieces if you prefer short lessons. For additional resources, visit www.CharacterFirstEd.com.

3 WAYS TO BUILD SELF-CONTROL:

Educate

Focus on self-control for a period of time. Use the lessons in this curriculum to talk about self-control and why it matters. Look for ways to emphasize self-control during other subjects, such as reading, math, language, history, social studies, science, music, health, and athletics.

Evaluate

Think about daily decisions in the light of good character. Ask yourself and your students, "Is this the right thing to do?" Use the "I Wills" on page 4 as behavioral objectives, and refer to these standards when correcting negative attitudes and behavior.

Celebrate

Catch people doing good and point out the character qualities they demonstrated. Children thrive on sincere encouragement, so don't overlook the little opportunities to praise each day!

Dr. Virginia Smith, president, Character First Ed.
Robert Greenlaw, writer

www.CharacterFirstEd.com
877. 357. 0001
Printed in the U.S.A.
Item: 04160

978-1-952938-25-2

DEFINE SELF-CONTROL
(Discussion, 15 minutes)

Point out and discuss key words in the definition. Review and commit the definition to memory. Use the Self-Control Character Card (sold separately) to remind or reward students who learn the definition.

Definition: *Choosing to do what is right, even when I don't feel like it.*

The word *self-control* combines the Old English *seolf* with the Latin *contra rotulus*, which means "against a roll." Just as a driver steers a car in the right direction by controlling the steering wheel, a person shows self-control by steering his or her actions in the right direction.

Imagine riding in a car that is out of control. It can be frightening and very dangerous! This is also true for people who are out of control. They can hurt themselves and other people.

Self-Control is like having steering and brakes in the journey of life. It means saying "no" to some things in order to say "yes" to something better.

Related concepts:
self-restraint, self-discipline, willpower, temperance, moderation

Discussion:
● How does an athlete show self-control in preparing for a game or race? Can you think of at least 5 examples of self-control?

● What are some ways you show self-control during a typical school day?

● What is the opposite of self-control? (Being impulsive, wild, rash, immature, manipulative, or self-indulging.)

● How can self-control help you feel healthier and happier?

"Self-control is the chief element in self-respect, and self-respect is the chief element in courage." —*Thucydides*

Additional resources at
www.CharacterFirstEd.com

RED LIGHT, GREEN LIGHT
(Project & Game, 25 minutes)

Use this hands-on project and optional game to remind students to control their actions.

Drivers must pay close attention to traffic lights in order to be safe. Do you know what each color means?

- A red light means *stop*.
- A yellow light means *caution*.
- A green light means *go ahead*.

Just as drivers need self-control to follow traffic lights, you need self-control to *stop* doing something wrong, *use caution* if you are not sure it is right, and *go ahead* with confidence when doing the right thing.

Make a traffic light using pieces of colored paper or download a template at www.CharacterFirstEd.com. Start with a black piece of paper, then glue or tape three circles to the front: red on top, yellow in the middle, and green on the bottom. Finish by writing the following words on each circle.

- Red = "Stop! Don't do it!"
- Yellow = "Caution! Think before you act!"
- Green = "Go! Do the right thing!"

Variations:
- Play the game "Red Light, Green Light" where students line up at one end of the room and only go when you say "Green Light." Anyone who moves after you say "Red Light" is out of the game.
- Use the traffic light theme to decorate a bulletin board for self-control.

MEALTIME MANNERS
(Exploration, 20 minutes)

Discuss how self-control can be applied at least three times a day—during mealtimes!

See how many mealtime manners your students can suggest. Design a poster or display for your classroom or cafeteria.

Suggested Manners:
- Chew with your mouth closed.
- Do not talk with food in your mouth.
- Wait for everyone to be served before eating.
- Ask someone to pass the food instead of demanding it.
- Wipe dirty hands on your napkin, not your clothes.
- Try not to burp, slurp, or make unnecessary noise.
- Do not talk about gross things at the table.
- Wait to be excused or dismissed.
- Thank the cook or host.
- Clean up after yourself.

Self-Control
Choosing to do what is right, even when I don't feel like it

3

Building Strong Character

Encourage students in the right direction by noticing "little things" that reflect good character. Don't overlook opportunities to recognize students for self-control when they:

- Sit still in class.
- Act calm instead of being wild.
- Raise their hands before talking.
- Use an "indoor voice" inside.
- Walk in the hall instead of running.
- Walk away from a conflict instead of fighting.
- Eat with good manners.
- Have good eye-contact when talking with adults.
- Say "excuse me" if they bump into someone.
- Wait patiently without getting upset.
- Handle books and school supplies gently instead of being rough with them.
- Report incidents of bullying instead of letting others get hurt.

I WILL...
(Discussion, 25 minutes)

1. Think before I act.
When tempted to do something wrong, think about the possible consequences and do the right thing. If you're not sure what to do, ask a parent, teacher, or counselor for advice.

- Why is it important to think before you act?
- Who could you talk to if you don't know what to do?

2. Control my temper.
Take time to "cool off" when you feel angry or upset. Don't throw a fit or take your anger out on others. Ask yourself, "Why do I feel this way?"

- How could you respond with self-control if someone pushes you in line?
- If you ask someone to stop bothering you and the person doesn't stop, what can you do next? What are your options?

3. Respect others and their belongings.
Every person deserves respect as a human being, no matter your differences. Don't make fun of others, call them names, or mess with their belongings.

- Why is it wrong to vandalize, litter, paint graffiti, or break what is not yours?
- How does bullying show disrespect toward others?
- How can you disagree with someone and still show respect?

4. Sit still and be quiet.
There are times to run around and times to sit still, times to play and times to be quiet and work. Self-control means doing the right thing at the right time.

- What does self-control "look like" in class?

5. Build healthy habits.
Self-control can help you eat, sleep, and exercise the right amount. It can also help you stay away from things that might damage your mind or body.

- Why is it important to take good care of your body?
- What should you do if someone offers you drugs or tries to touch you inappropriately? Why should you *not* keep these things secret?

STICKS AND STONES
(Project, 25 minutes)

Use this project as a reminder to choose words carefully— words that will build up instead of tear down.

You have probably heard the saying, "Sticks and stones may break my bones, but words will never hurt me." The truth is that words *do* hurt, and they can hurt very deeply.

The good news is that words can also build up and encourage others, which is the point of this activity. Give each student a half-sheet of paper to fold in half. Staple the sides to form a pocket, and write "Words of Encouragement" on the front.

Cut another half-sheet of paper into strips, and on each strip write an encouraging word or phrase, such as "Thank you," or "Good job," or "I appreciate you." See how many positive words the students can write down and place inside their paper pockets. Occasionally review these words as a reminder to choose words carefully.

Supplies: paper, scissors, stapler, pens or pencils

MAKE 'EM LAUGH!
(Project, 15 minutes)

This activity is a silly but helpful way to build self-control by *not* laughing, even if you really feel like laughing.

Let one or more students volunteer to be in "the hot seat" with other students standing around them. Give the class one minute to try and get the volunteers to laugh. Meanwhile, the volunteers should try to NOT laugh, as a way to practice self-control. Explain to the class that they cannot touch or tickle the volunteers in any way. If the volunteer laughs, stop the activity and discuss how difficult it can be to show self-control, but with practice we can get better at it.

Variations:
- Have students stare at a certain object or practice writing letters on a sheet of paper while you try to distract them— which builds self-control in their focus and fine motor skills.
- Practice walking around the classroom or building very quietly, which builds self-control in large motor skills.

CONTROL YOUR TEMPER
(Exploration, 25 minutes)

This object lesson emphasizes the importance of controlling your temper.

Have you ever seen someone out of control? It is similar to a volcano—people get hurt, things get broken, and it takes a long time to repair the damage.

Self-control means controlling your emotions instead of losing your temper. Never hit people, break things, or throw a tantrum when things don't go your way.

To illustrate this danger, mix equal parts of vinegar and water to fill about half of a 2 liter soda bottle. Place a teaspoon of baking soda into a piece of tissue or napkin, and tie it closed with a string. The tied bundle should fit through the neck of the bottle.

Drop the bundle into the solution and cork the bottle with a snug-fitting cork. (Do NOT screw on the soda bottle cap). Aim the bottle in a direction where no damage can occur when the speeding cork pops off.

Warning: This activity is best done outside. Always use safety precautions such as protective eyewear. Keep students a safe distance from the bottle.

 # SELF-CONTROL POEM
(Literacy Connection, 15 minutes)

Teach this poem as a way to memorize the five "I Wills." Watch the video at www.CharacterFirstEd.com.

I will always think before I act. I'll practice sitting still.
I will eat the things I really need and stop when I am filled.

I will use the best of manners. And if I get all upset,
I will not burst out with anger, but will keep myself in check.

My character is what will make a leader out of me!
So next time through, let's say it more ENTHUSIASTICALLY!

Additional activities at
www.CharacterFirstEd.com

Abigail Adams

A salty breeze blew gently into her face as she watched Boston harbor slowly fade into the distance. Abigail Adams, her daughter, Nabby, and two friends were on their way to Europe to see Abigail's husband and son who had been gone seven years.

Abigail and Nabby's cabin was just eight feet wide, with barely enough room between the beds to turn around. It was quite a change from their large farmhouse in Braintree, near Boston.

Living conditions on the ship grew worse and worse. But instead of blowing her temper or losing control, Abigail found something useful to do. She rolled up her sleeves and began cleaning the ship herself!

After one month at sea, the ship finally reached England. The weary passengers disembarked and lodged in a nearby inn. What had started out as a miserable journey ended quite happily.

After years of separation and a tiring journey across the ocean, Abigail was finally reunited with her husband and son.

Read the full story about Abigail Adams' journey at www.CharacterFirstEd.com.

Learn how the Black Bear demonstrates self-control as it prepares each year for winter hibernation.

THE BLACK BEAR
(Story, 20 minutes)

Two men stood in the snow. One held a set of binoculars, and the other pointed a small, black box across the rolling landscape, as if searching for something. From the box they heard *Beep, Beep, Beep, Beep, BEEEEEEEEEEEEEPPP!*

"She's over there!" said one of the men pointing toward a fallen tree that was mostly covered with snow. The men waded through the snow until they came to the base of the tree. They started digging around the tangled roots until they uncovered a chamber about three feet high and five feet wide, hidden in the midst of the tangled roots.

There, wedged against the back wall of the chamber, was a female black bear hibernating through the winter. The two men were naturalists who were studying the life and health of animals they had tagged with radio transmitters the previous summer. That's how they found the bear.

But the bear wasn't alone. Just a week before, she gave birth to two baby cubs who were hardly bigger than a tea cup and weighed less than a pound each. Small and helpless, the cubs would never survive the harsh conditions outside the den. But inside the den, they were warm and safe thanks to the preparations their mother had made a few months before.

Watch Your Diet
When food becomes scarce in the winter, black bears stop eating and enter their dens for a long winter sleep. Before hibernation, bears eat as much as 18 pounds of food per day. Then they stop eating for months!

Sometimes it's hard to stop eating or to eat the right things. For the black bear, this comes naturally—but for us, it takes self-control!

Get Along With Others
The black bear is the most numerous species of bear in North America. The color of its coat varies from shiny black in the east to cinnamon brown in the west, and some bears are nearly white.

Black bears rarely confront or attack humans. They usually avoid human contact altogether, preferring to climb a tree or find some other escape. Black bears also rarely fight with one another.

Sometimes it's hard to stay calm and not get upset when things don't go your way. For the black bear, this comes naturally—but for us, it takes self-control!

Get Your Sleep

As winter approaches, black bears start searching for a suitable den where they can curl up and lie down. Even though they could keep roaming the woods, they enter their dens at the right time and go to sleep.

Sometimes it's hard to stop what you're doing and go to bed on time. But that's what helps you wake up on time and feel rested! For the black bear, this comes naturally—but for us, it takes self-control.

Calm Down

As the snow piles up around the den, it helps insulate the bear from the cold wind. To conserve energy, the bear's heart rate lowers from 40 beats per minute to only 8 beats per minute. It even slows its breathing to just one breath every 45 seconds.

Sometimes it's hard to calm down, sit still, and focus on your work. Sometimes it's hard to control all your energy. For the black bear, this comes naturally—but for us, it takes self-control.

Wake Up!

Bears in the north generally sleep more deeply than bears farther south, and the length of their hibernation depends on how long winter lasts in their area. Nevertheless, black bears can still wake up in the middle of winter and come out of their dens if they are disturbed.

Sometimes it's hard to wake up and get out of bed when you feel like going back to sleep. For the black bear, waking up on time comes naturally—but for us, it takes self-control.

Follow the black bear's example to control your eating, sleeping, playing, and working. Make the choice to do what's right, and you'll be glad you did.

 Watch a video of the self-control story at www.CharacterFirstEd.com. Also download a coloring sheet of the black bear and other activity pages.

OVERVIEW: **A car that drifts out-of-control is dangerous to everyone in its path—and to everyone inside the car.** Similarly, losing control over your temper, emotions, or will-power can cause a lot of unnecessary pain. Self-control means steering your life in a positive direction and doing what is right. When you say "no" to one thing, think of it as saying "yes" to something better—something that can help you reach your goals!

Self-Control

Definition: Choosing to do what is right, even when I don't feel like it

I WILL...

❏ **Think before I act.**
❏ **Control my temper.**
❏ **Respect others and their belongings.**
❏ **Sit still and be quiet.**
❏ **Build healthy habits.**

The Black Bear demonstrates self-control as it prepares each year for winter hibernation. The bear stops eating, slows its breathing, and lowers its heart rate while it sleeps.

CHARACTER QUIZ:

1. Why is it important to do what is right, even when you don't feel like it? _____

2. What could happen to someone who has very little self-control? _____

3. Self-control includes: **a.** going to bed on time. **b.** not over-eating. **c.** showing good manners. **d.** all of the above.

4. Self-control means you never have any fun: TRUE? or FALSE?

5. What are some healthy habits that can make you a stronger person? _____

6. Athletes make a lot of sacrifices in order to reach their goals. Can you think of ways athletes show self-control or self-discipline?
_____

cf
characterfirst.
education